MathStart®
COUNTING BY 2s, 3s, AND 4s

Spunky Monkeys on Parade

by Stuart J. Murphy

illustrated by Lynne Cravath

HarperCollinsPublishers

LEVEL
2

In memory of S.L.T.
and all our spunky Fourth of July parades.
—S.J.M.

To my big little monkey, Jeff, with love!
—L.C.

The publishers and author would like to thank
teachers Patricia Chase, Phyllis Goldman, and
Patrick Hopfensperger for their help
in making the math in MathStart just right for kids.

HarperCollins®, ✿®, and MathStart® are registered trademarks of HarperCollins Publishers.
For more information about the MathStart series, write to HarperCollins Children's Books,
10 East 53rd Street, New York, NY 10022.

Bugs incorporated in the MathStart series design were painted by Jon Buller.

Spunky Monkeys on Parade
Text copyright © 1999 by Stuart J. Murphy
Illustrations copyright © 1999 by Lynne W. Cravath
Printed in the U.S.A. All rights reserved.
Visit our web site at http://www.harperchildrens.com.

Library of Congress Cataloging-in-Publication Data
Murphy, Stuart J., date
  Spunky monkeys on parade / by Stuart J. Murphy ; illustrated by Lynne Cravath.
    p.   cm. — (MathStart)
  "Counting by 2s, 3s, and 4s, Level 2."
  Summary: In the Monkey Day Parade, monkey majorettes, cyclists, tumblers, and band members create
a spectacle as they move along in groups of two, three, and four.
  ISBN 006-028014-X. — ISBN 0-06-028015-8 (lib. bdg.).— ISBN 0-06-446727-9 (pbk.)
  [1. Monkeys—Fiction.   2. Parades—Fiction.   3. Counting.   4. Stories in rhyme.]   I. Cravath, Lynne
Woodstock, ill.   II. Title.   III. Series.
PZ8.3.M935Sp   1999
[E]—dc21   98-6936
                                                                                                            CIP
                                                                                                            AC

Typography by Elynn Cohen
1 2 3 4 5 6 7 8 9 10
❖
First Edition

Today's the Monkey Day Parade.
The marshal marches by.

The monkey majorette comes next.
Her baton flies way up high.

The cycling monkeys follow—
just watch those monkeys ride!

Together they pop wheelies,
two cyclists side by side.

11

There go . . .

2 4 6 8 10

12   14   16   18   20

. . . monkeys riding by.

Here come the monkey tumblers.
They cartwheel everywhere.

Three by three, they somersault
and leap up in the air.

17

There go . . .

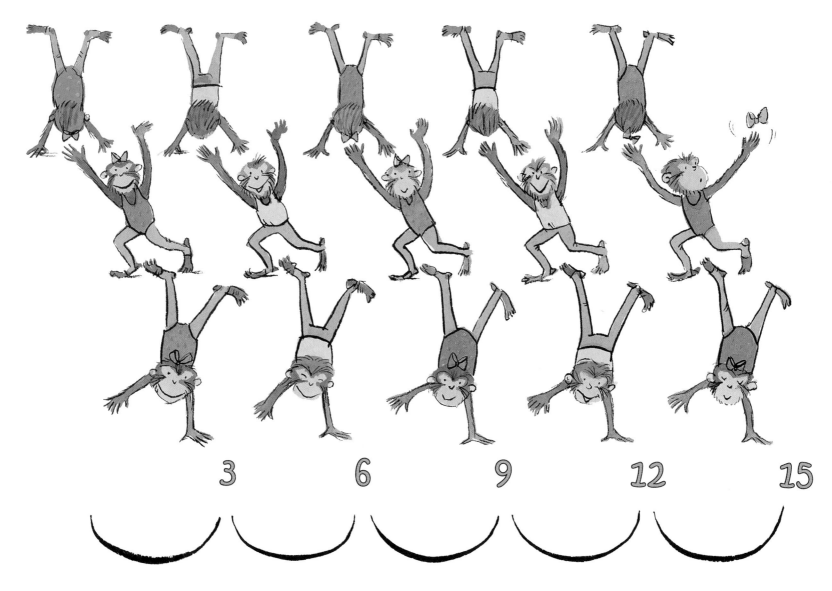

3　　　6　　　9　　　12　　　15

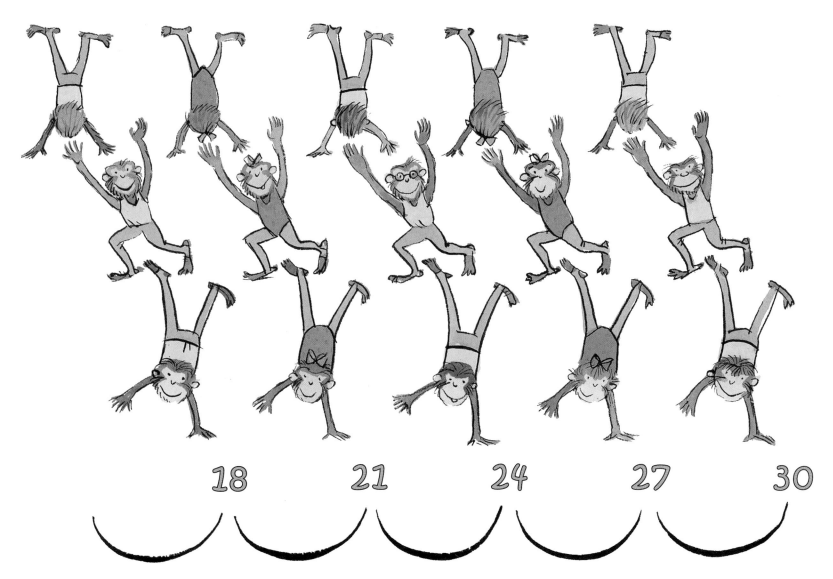

18   21   24   27   30

. . . monkeys tumbling by.

The monkey band starts marching.
The musicians kick their feet.

Count the drummers—four across.
Rat-a-tat's their beat.

There go . . .

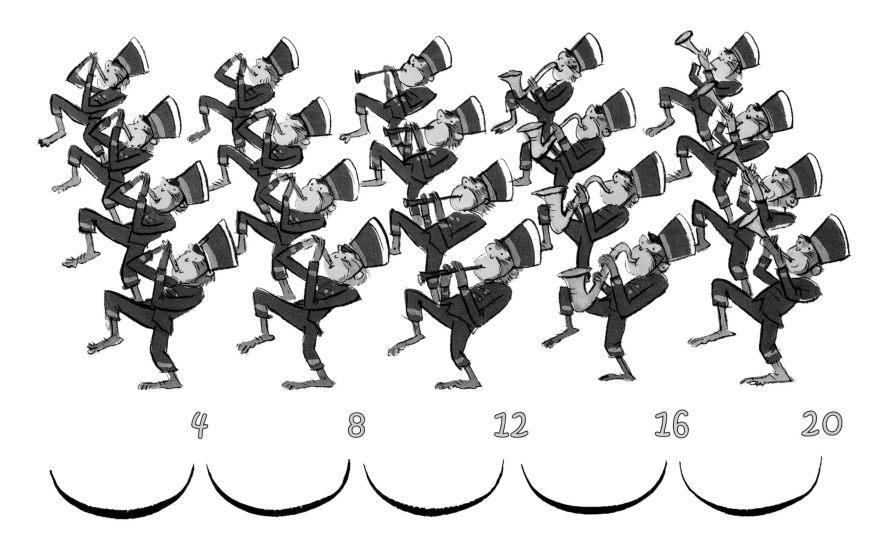

4   8   12   16   20

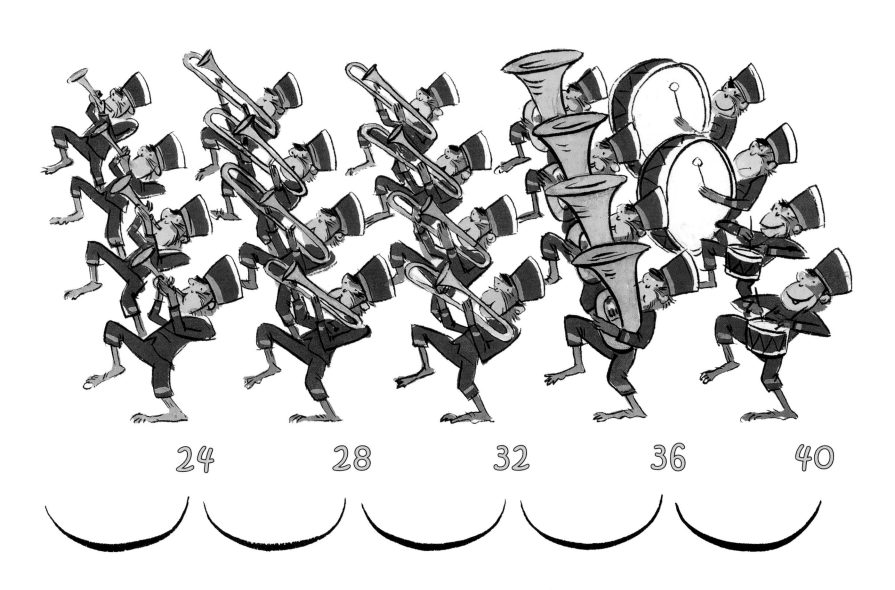

24   28   32   36   40

. . . monkeys marching by.

At last the monkey float arrives.
The cheering grows so loud!

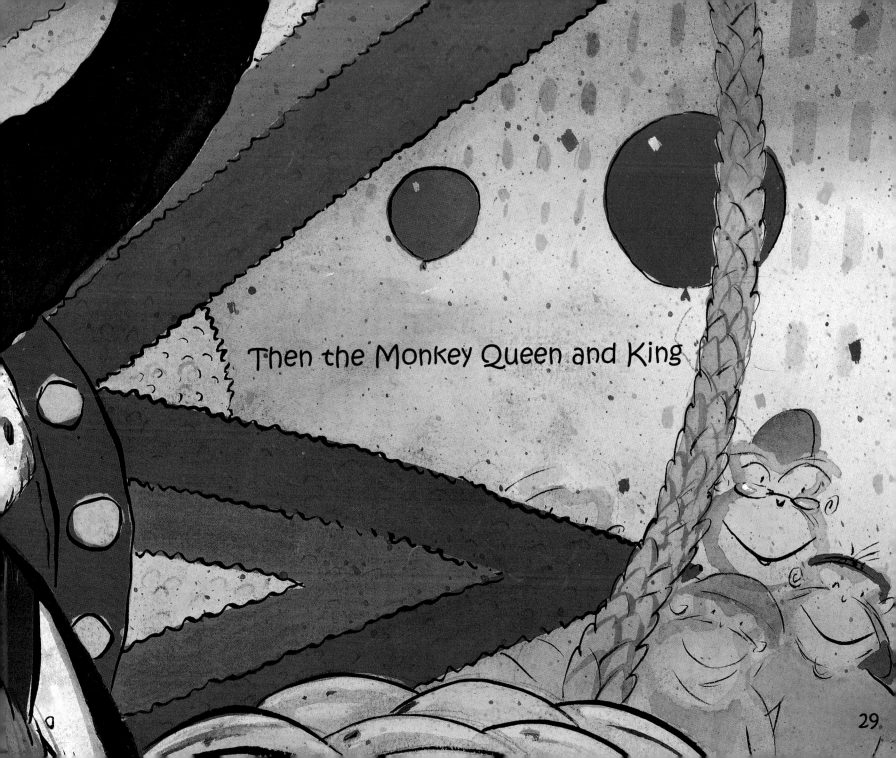

Then the Monkey Queen and King

throw bananas to the crowd.

In *Spunky Monkeys on Parade*, the math concept is counting by 2s, 3s, and 4s. (This is called skip counting.) Counting by numbers greater than one is a first step in the development of multiplication skills.

If you would like to have more fun with the math concepts presented in *Spunky Monkeys on Parade*, here are a few suggestions:

- Read the story with your child and talk about what is going on in each picture. Encourage the child to interact with the illustrations and count the monkeys aloud as you read.

- Reread the story together and have the child count monkeys by 2s, 3s, or 4s, and then count by 1s to see that the total is the same.

- Ask if the monkey cyclists could go in rows of 3s or 4s instead. Would the rows come out even? Then try this same activity with the tumblers and the musicians.

- Teach the calculator to count by 2s, 3s, and 4s. With most calculators you can enter the following keystrokes to count by 2s: 0 + 2 = = = = =. Have the child count the number of keystrokes necessary to count to 36 by 2s, 3s, and 4s.

Following are some activities that will help you extend the concepts presented in *Spunky Monkeys on Parade* into a child's life:

Shopping: While shopping in the supermarket, help your child find objects that are packaged in 2s, 3s, or 4s, like lightbulbs, paper towels, or sticks of margarine or butter. Skip count to find the total number of items on the shelf.

At Home: Find things around the house that come in 2s, 3s, and 4s, like shoes and mittens, silverware settings, or chair and table legs. Ask, "How many chair legs are there in the kitchen?" or "How many pieces of silverware are there on the table?"

Stringing Beads: You will need beads of two different colors (for example, red and yellow) and three strings. On the first string, have the child string 2 red beads, 1 yellow, 2 red, and so on. On the second string, arrange 3 red beads, 1 yellow, 3 red, and so on. On the third string, arrange 4 red beads, 1 yellow, 4 red, and so on. Compare the three strings. Which one has more red beads?

The following stories include similar concepts to those that are presented in *Spunky Monkeys on Parade*:

- WHAT COMES IN 2'S, 3'S, & 4'S? by Suzanne Aker

- COUNTING BY KANGAROOS by Joy N. Hulme

- ARCTIC FIVES ARRIVE by Elinor J. Pinczes